NUMEROLOGY: A PRACTICAL GUIDE

Gain Clarity in Your Life, Embrace

Easy-to-Apply Remedies, Enhance Your

Success Rate, and Transform Your Life

with Numerology's Wisdom

DR. ARUN KUMAAR KHANDA
https://arunkumarrk.com

YOUR FREE GIFT

As a token of my gratitude for taking out time to read my book, I would like to offer you a free gift. Click the below link or scan the QR code to download your free eBook PDF

https://arun-kumar-khanda.ck.page/00c46de54c

Acknowledgments

In my journey as an author, I have been blessed with support that has significantly contributed to my success. I am deeply grateful to my mentor and bestselling author, Mr. Som Bathla, for his mentorship, motivation, and guidance in writing, self-publishing, and launching my books, which has been crucial on my path to becoming an author-entrepreneur.

I also extend my heartfelt thanks to my author community, especially to Sooraj Achar, a bestselling author himself, for his timely technical support, encouragement, and invaluable advice, which have made my work much easier.

My gratitude goes out to my readers for their unwavering support. I am also thankful for this incredible platform that provides authors with the resources needed to transform the lives of millions.

Thank you all for being a part of this journey. Readers can connect with me at akkhanda9@gmail.com.

Sincerely,

Arun Kumaar Khanda

TABLE OF CONTENTS

WHY TO READ THIS BOOK?

1. Unlock Personal Insights:

This book provides a deep understanding of how numbers influence your personality, relationships, and life choices. By learning about your numeroscope, you can gain valuable self-awareness and make decisions that truly align with who you are.

2. Practical Solutions for Life's Challenges:

Every problem has a solution. This book gives a wide range of solutions for missing numbers and offers actionable steps to bring balance and harmony into your life. These easy-to-follow practices can help you overcome obstacles and enhance your strengths.

3. Enhance Your Relationships:

Whether you're exploring the significance of your name or considering the numerology of marriage, this book provides insights that can improve your personal and professional relationships. It's a powerful tool for creating more meaningful connections.

4. Simple and Effective Remedies:

The book introduces natural elements and daily rituals that are inexpensive and easy to incorporate into your routine. These remedies, based on ancient wisdom, help you align with universal energies and create a more balanced, fulfilling life.

5. Empower Your Future:

"Numerology: A Practical Guide" isn't just about numbers; it's about using this knowledge to take control of your destiny. With practical advice and clear explanations, this book empowers you to make choices that lead to success and happiness.

Chapter one

INTRODUCTION

"Numbers are the language of the universe, and numerology is the Rosetta Stone."

-Unknown

Welcome to my second book of this series on numerology. My first book **"Unlock Your Destiny with Numerology"** is doing well. That book discusses the basic concepts of numerology and the game of numbers. The contents include the origins of numerology in different belief systems and its type. What is Loshu Grid? How can you independently prepare your numeroscope? What are MOOLANKA (root number), BHAGYANKA (destiny number), and Kua number? How can you able to find out these numbers from your date of birth? How do different numbers combined with other numbers create Yogas in your Numeroscope? What are the compatibilities of numbers? The lucky and unlucky numbers in respect of a numeroscope and many more ideas and concepts have been discussed.

You are here, which indicates that you are interested in numerology and ready to transform your life.

NUMBERS ARE PART AND PARCEL OF YOUR LIFE.

Numbers are present everywhere. Hans Decoz says;

"Numbers are the language of the universe, and through numerology, we can understand the deeper meanings of our lives."

Can you deny the presence of numbers in your life? Because from your birth to your death, even for every incarnation, numbers are with you. It will remain with you for an indefinite period till you get solvation. You can't deny it. Numbers and you appear to be inseparable. Remember numbers are the language of the universe and you are the product of the universe. How can numbers leave you alone? We have to find the energy possessed by numbers and harness them for our optimum benefits.

In numerology, nine numbers starting from 1 to 9 are used to calculate the destiny of an individual. Zero is never used in numerology, unlike mathematics.

1 is the number that represents the **SUN.**

2 is the number that represents the **MOON.**

3 is the number that represents **JUPITER.**

4 is the number that represents **RAHU**

5 is the number that represents **MERCURY.**

6 is the number that represents **VENUS.**

7 is the number that represents **KETU.**

8 is the number that represents **SATURN.**

9 is the number that represents **MARS.**

In astrology, you can find all of the above planets and their effects on the horoscope. But in numerology, we use numbers to predict the future. Some planets are friends to each other and some are treated each other as enemies. Some planets behave neutrally. You are no doubt familiar with our social scenario, some behave friendly some act like enemies and few don't care about our cause, the same principles apply in numerology. Why? Because we all are connected to the same energy source, some say that is infinite intelligence. We all are there in one photo frame.

HAVE YOU EVER THOUGHT YOUR DATE OF BIRTH IS SPECIAL?

Have you ever thought that you are unique and the secret is hiding in your date of birth? If you have not treated yourself special to date, you have done injustice to yourself.

"Love yourself first, and everything else falls into line." - Camila Cabello

From now start loving yourself. It is called self-love, the unique one where you may not have to pay anything but to attend to yourself. You might have faced obstacles and setbacks in your life. Might have been disappointed with your fortune. You might have visited the astrologers but in vain. Believe me, the secret of your success is hiding in your date of birth. No date of birth is good or bad. God has given enough to you, but you could not find the diamond from it. Don't worry I will tell you the secret of your date of birth. Find out the best from it for your transformation. It will definitely reduce your struggle. Give a big smile on your face and increase your happiness and well-being.

Let you try the concept of numerology in your life and see what happens. Knowledge is everywhere in the books, in our teachers, and on the internet. But unless you know the way to utilize it for excellence, the same knowledge is useless for you.

Let me tell you some of the secrets of your date of birth. In every date of birth, there are 81 combinations of MOOLANKA and BHAGYANKA. They indicate your life path and direction. I have discussed it in my first book in detail.

When we prepare a Numeroscope or birth chart from your date of birth, you cannot find the presence of all the 9 numbers, unlike a horoscope. You can find some numbers are present and some are missing from the date of birth. It is said out of one million one birth chat can witness the presence of all 9 numbers in the chart. It is definitely the rarest of rare events.

You can find eight types of lines and eight types of Yogas in the Lo-Shu Grid. From the grid, we find the strengths and weaknesses of the individual. Now you can ask how you can find the hidden treasure from the chart. How can you overcome the weakness of your birth chart?

Numerology can explain everything you want to know.

You can find the missing numbers from your date of birth. The missing numbers indicate you are missing something in your life. But nothing to worry about. Every problem has a solution.

"Every problem has a solution; it may sometimes just need another perspective." - Katherine Russell

Yes, I have answers to all your questions. When diagnosis is made, then treatment is easy. We can do remedies for the missing numbers. Believe me, you are unique and the remedies will make you unstoppable. You can explore your strengths and overcome your weaknesses without much expenditure and effort.

Can you imagine your name spelling may foil your plan if not done according to your birth chart? Have you ever heard before that mere name spelling can change your fortune?

Yes, different case studies suggest that 30-40% of your success or failure depends on your name spelling. If your name spelling is corrected according to your birth date you may get 30-40% more success in your life. I myself have corrected my name spelling and getting the benefit.

Further, we can predict your future years, months, and dates. Future predictions can help you to make better decisions for better predictions in your life.

WHAT IS THERE FOR YOU IN THIS BOOK?

This book discusses the importance of numbers, repetitive numbers, and their impact on your life, creativity, profession, and marriage life. How the missing numbers are creating a vacuum within your workspace.

How to make your life beautiful with different remedies. How to perform better in your profession. How to achieve your dream job and crush your goals with small remedies without much spending or changing some small habits. The magical combinations of numbers can give you a better insight into your life for a better course of action.

In our time marriage is definitely an issue to be addressed systematically with love and empathy. You can easily detect from your birth chart, whether you are going for love or an arranged marriage. A master stroke-like name spelling correction can amaze you and unfold your success rate.

The beauty of numerology is it only needs a date of birth, no day, time, or place of birth is required, unlike astrology.

Do you believe one can choose it as a profession? The answer is Yes if you go deeper and be trained properly. If you give proper attention and do hard as well as smart work you can earn lakhs of rupees per month. If you are in a good profession and happy then no issue, you may use it as your passive income.

You can implement the science of numerology in your life for your perfection. Remember no one is perfect on this planet. Everyone has the scope to improve.   Capacity building and acquiring knowledge give anyone more power. You can use it for the improvement of your family members like your parents, wife/husband, children, friends, and relatives. Can you imagine a small piece of advice that may do wonders in anyone's life? Can put a smile on the lips of many. Then why not implement it? Remember, learning is a continuous process and empowerment is your choice.

Chapter two

IMPACT OF REPETITIVE NUMBER IN NUMEROSCOPE

"In numerology, nothing happens by accident. The numbers are here to guide us on our path."

– Anonymous

I think you all are familiar with Lo-Shu Grid and numeroscope. You might have prepared one or more numeroscopes and have an idea about the presence of repetitive numbers in the birth chart. But you might be confused about the presence of repetitive numbers in the birth chart. One number may come once or even 4 to five times. The prediction of the future may differ according to the presence of numbers. It is definitely interesting to know the magic of the repetitive number.

Impact of repetitive number

The general observations of the repetitive numbers represent the following characters.

- If a number comes once its strength is not up to mark.

- If a number comes twice its strength becomes maximum.

- If a number comes thrice its strength exaggerates.

- If a number comes to quadruple (fourth time) its power becomes negative and the person may suffer from over sensitiveness or depression.

1 Represents Communication.

You are well known that in numerology 1 to 9 are used and not given any value to 0. Now let me tell you the impact of repetitive numbers for 1.

Once 1(1): Good communication skills but may not express own thoughts in an articulated manner.

Twice 1(11): The best communicator. Can express own thoughts in an impressive and articulated manner. The people with twice one is impartial and attractive.

Thrice 1(111): Communication is good but may turn into a chatterbox. If not(chatterbox) they become introverted and speak less. Further, depending on the demands of the situation they can act accordingly, but most of the time they are chatterboxes. They often feel ashamed to ask for their own needs.

Quadruple 1(1111): Communication is not a problem but is paradoxical. They are introverted and often misunderstood without any fault for their expressions of emotion. Controversies follow them.

Quintuple 1(11111): Communication is good but controversies and paradoxes follow them. However, they can earn a name and fame in society in a bigger sphere.

For example, Amitav Bachan, a superstar actor in the Hindi film industry and host of Kaun Banega Crorepati, a reality show. Let us prepare his birth chart. His date of birth is 11.10.1942

4	9	22
	111111	

M-2, B-1, K-1

2 Represents Sensitivity and Intuitions.

Once 2(2): They are sensitive people and are intuitive. But ignore their own intuitions. They could not understand how much they would be.

Twice 2(22): They are very sensitive and intuitive. They should trust their intuition as what they say happens. They get the prior hints about the future happenings. They sometimes behave very seriously and never tolerate even friendly jokes. Goddess Saraswati lives on their tongues.

Thrice or more 2(222 or 2222): They are over-sensitive and intuitive. What they say it happens. They like loneliness. The children coming under such numbers are very sensitive. **Parents to be extra vigilant on the behavioral changes and attitudes of their kids. They should spend quality time with them, as there is every possibility that their kids may come under the spell of depression.** The people of such a combination may experience depression once or more times in their life span.

3 Represents Imagination and Creativity

Three once (3): They are creative and imaginative. Without imagination, one can't become effectively creative. They are considered good starters but can't finish the task as expected. They feel proud of their knowledge, which may lead to their failure and frustration.

Three twice (33): They are at best of imagination and creativity. The Imagination makes them good poets, writers, lyrists, and musicians. They sometimes become proud of their creativity. They don't care about the established social norms and go on their own path. The people may be good starters and bad finishers.

Three thrice (333): They can sell their dreams smartly and think knowledgeful and the best. They are creative, imaginative and excel in their lives in music, art, and writing poems.

Three Quadruple (3333): This combines found rare. The people are very imaginative and daydreamers. Dreams more act less. They can show you the stars during the daytime. They can clin bowled you with their creative dreams. You may get ready to purchase the Taj Mahal from them.

4 Represents Discipline and Organization

One four (4): They love discipline and are capable of running or handling an organization. They prefer to work by themselves and love hands-on activities. They respect the time most. They believe "the time and tide wait for non" proverb in true spirit. *They can be good painters, sculptors, cooks, and artisans.*

Twice four (44): They are super disciplined. Can create order out of chaos. They are resilient people and love hands-on activities. They may become renowned painters, sculptors, and artisans. For example, Leonardo da Vinci (Date of Birth 15.04.1452)

Thrice or Quadruple 4(444/4444): They are over disciplined and organized. Spend most of their valuable time in unnecessary arguments, and misunderstanding with others. They spend more time in the wrong fields and bite the dust with unsuccess. They struggle despite their talents for their super disciplined character.

5 Represents Emotional Balance.

Once 5(5): They are the blessed child of the infinite intelligence. They maintain a great balance in money, career, and relationships. They are resilient people and often bounce back from adversities. The people who have 5 on their birth chart should help others. If helped the beneficiary can enhance his talent or capabilities by up to 40%.

Twice 5(55): They are the assets of the society. They often help to the society. No doubt they are lazy but good performers. They understand their duties and responsibilities well. To start a work is their choice. They give more output in minimum time. **They are self-responsible and self-accountable.** They may not tolerate external interference in their work, can't handle pressure, and keep resignation letters in their pockets. They are good at heart and romantic people. Love marriage is their first preference.

Thrice or Quadruple 5(555/5555): They speak unwittingly. Can't handle the pressure. They are over-adventurous and prone to accidents.

6 Represents Home and Family.

Once 6(6): They are well connected to family and children. A sense of insecurity about their children always strikes their minds. Negative thoughts about their family nest in their minds.

Twice 6(66): They are obsessed with their children, wife, parents, etc. They often want their children to follow their own directions and directives. The real growth of their children is hindered due to such a type of approach. They remain in negative thoughts about their children without thinking about the worth of their children.

Thrice or quadruple 6(666/6666): They are much obsessed with their children, and family. Their minds are preoccupied with negative thoughts about children and wives. Their thoughts may cause the failure of their children's missions or fortune. Somebody rightly says; **"A parent's thoughts can either build up or tear down a child's future." – Unknown**

7   Represents   Disappointment   & Spiritualism.

Once seven (7): They are likely to be betrayed in love and marriage. The health, career, and money sectors also face the same issue. They may face emotional setbacks in their daily life. On the bright side, they are spiritual and problem solvers. They can excel if they prefer occult, reccy, numerology, Vastu, etc. as a profession.

Twice seven (77): There is every possibility of love marriage. They may be betrayed in their personal and love life. Emotional setbacks may be apprehended. They believe in scientific analysis of everything. Research, education, occult, and Vastu may be the right professions for them to excel. A note of advice for them- **"Not to trust anyone blindly."**

Thrice seven (777): They are prone to betrayal in love more than once. They are attracted to the opposite sex. If not attracted to the opposite sex, then they are attracted to spiritualism. Pre-marital or extramarital relationships are common for such types of people. They are emotionally tortured and remain unhappy without success and fulfillment. Marriage life is no less than a disaster for them. Research and the occult are the most suited professions for them.

Quadruple Seven (7777): Love life is a nemesis for them. **They go for multiple marriages without fruitful conjugal life. Extramarital relationships are the benchmark for such types of people.** They run after astrologers with the hope of rectifying their lifeline but in vain. Life takes a new turn after 50 years. They submerge in spiritualism and become saints.

8 Represents Money and Financial Management.

Once eight (8): They are good at money and financial management. Keep money in multiple places and have multiple bank accounts. Don't trust others easily without proper verification and validation. Money and financial sectors can suit them for opting as professions.

Twice eight (88): They never trust anyone easily without proper verifications. Witness slow progress in their lives. They are excellent at managing money and finance sectors in their lives. They can do excellent in their jobs in the money, banking, and financial sectors. An MBA in finance may be an excellent choice for them.

Triple/ quadruple eight (888/8888): They are egoistic and never believe anyone. The success rate decreases with the increase of number 8. They maintain multiple bank accounts and are very good at financial management. All the works are delayed. Jobs in the finance and money sectors are good for them.

9 Represents Humanism.

Single 9(9): They are intelligent and humanitarian. They respect human sentiments and are empathetic in their approach. Never disrespect anyone and are sympathetic.

Double 9(99): No doubt they are very very intelligent and sensitive. They are egoistic but remain in readiness to help. In their thinking they are intelligent.

Triple 9(999): They are over-intelligent but behave to be supreme and underestimate others. However, they help others in their time of need. Their stubborn nature makes them enemies. They also search for an opportunity to settle scores against opponents.

Quadruple/quintuples 9(9999/99999): They never understand their own worth and talents. Act like **"I am the best."** They are angry in nature and underestimate others. Never try to make friends or share happiness or sorrows with others. Self-ego makes them lonely.

Now you are aware of the impact of the presence of numbers in the birth chart and the characters of the people coming under the influence of the numbers. Now proceed to the next chapter.

Conclusion:

Understanding the impact of repetitive numbers in your numeroscope offers valuable insights into your personality and life path. Each number carries its own energy and influence, which can be either a source of strength or a challenge. It depends on how frequently it appears in your chart. While the presence of these numbers can amplify positive traits, they can also push certain characteristics to extremes, leading to potential struggles. By recognizing these patterns, you gain a deeper awareness of yourself. You can do better to overcome the challenges by making informed decisions that align with your true nature. This knowledge empowers you to harness the strengths of your numbers while being mindful of the areas where balance is needed. As you move forward, let this understanding guide you toward a more harmonious and fulfilling life. Remember only awareness may not help to get success in life unless you take proactive steps to overcome the challenges.

Chapter three

IMPACT OF MISSING NUMBERS

"Your life is a reflection of the numbers you vibrate to."

– Hans Decoz (a well-known numerologist and author)

Every number has to play a role in our lives. You know that our numeroscope is prepared as per the guiding principles of La-Shu Grid. While preparing your birth chart, you might find that some numbers are missing from your numeroscope. You might be excited to know about the missing numbers from your birth chart. What sort of impact can it have on your life? What are the remedies or alternate numbers present to complement the missing numbers and many more things? Are you ready to know the secrets of the missing numbers? Join me on this journey of personal transformation and acquiring knowledge.

Missing Number: 1

One is the sun, the king of the planetary system. If the king is missing what would happen to your life? You must be excited to know about this. Let me explain in simple language. One represents communication. If one is missing, people may face problems in communicating their thoughts and messages. They don't have any attractive personalities. Have no self-ego. They may be stammerer. But can make friends with others easily.

Missing Number: 2

Two represent intuitions and sensitivity. If the 2 is missing from your birth chart you shall be non-sensitive to others. You may become rude on some occasions. You will not be able to be intuitive in your life. You may do wrong but despite admitting your mistakes you try to justify it.

Missing Number: 3

3 represents creativity and imagination. Can you imagine a life without creative awareness and imagination? Without dreams in their eyes? What is the value of a life without a dream? Only the reality of hard tasks? They are not resilient people but surrender to their circumstances. They may

experience emotional and financial issues without finding any solutions.

Missing Number: 4

4 is a symbol of discipline and organization. How can you win the race in your life without discipline? We have been taught that discipline is a key indicator of success in our lives. Discipline means self-discipline, discipline in our day-to-day life. Discipline in our workspace. Discipline in our relationships and so on.

"The only discipline that lasts is self-discipline." — Bum Phillips

Similarly, 4 represents the organization, which means arranging elements systematically to achieve any goal. Without discipline, you may not be organized, and without organization, you may not achieve your goals. Now you understand how 4 is important in your birth chat.

Missing Number: 5

5 is a symbol of balance. It represents mercury. If you can remember the Lo-Shu Grid, you can see the position of 5 at the center of the table. Now you can imagine if the center point of the grid is missing means, your life is disturbed. You may struggle to earn, relationships, personal and professional life.

But, never be disappointed remedies are there to redress the issues.

Missing Number: **6**

6 represents social bonding, love, and affection. It is a number of relationships, the essence of human existence. Can you imagine a world where nobody is yours? No love, no children, no sharing of sorrow and happiness. It is a very disappointing and unpleasant journey in life. Then what is the effect on the persons having no 6? They help others but nobody comes forward to help them in time of need. If married no good love life with their better half. If have children, they may not care for their parents. During old age, the people are not cared for or respected by their children. They may find their fortune in old age homes. But don't be disappointed, we have remedies for this missing number.

Missing Number: **7**

This is a number of disappointments. If it is missing, then one positive thing for the people is that they will not be betrayed in love and social life. But they may be less educated. Belief in religion and spiritualism may be missing from their life path. They may be devoid of wisdom and research work limiting their scope in life.

Missing Number: **8**

8 is a number of money and finance. What do you mean by this money and finance? Can one live without money and financial management in his life? How can he survive without food, shelter, clothing, and health care without money? It is almost difficult to survive without money and its proper management. Now you can guess what would be the life of a person without 8 in his birth chart. His struggle to earn money continues throughout his life. He may face problems in financial management if earned money. He may spend money without proper application of his mind and face a financial crisis.

Missing Number: **9**

It represents memory and intelligence. If 9 is missing the person may not remember things easily. He has to make more effort to remember things. He may be a backbencher in his class. You may not get the desired respect and behavior from him. He may not behave properly with friends, family members, and colleagues.

Are you now eagerly waiting to know the remedies to fill up the gap created by the missing numbers? Am I right? I can understand your pain. Life is yours, and you have to magnify it with proper remedies. I can only suggest you but you have to take action. Now see the complementary numbers.

Complementary Numbers.

Do you know, what is called a complementary number in numerology? A complementary number is a number that balances or enhances another number's energy. It can act on behalf of its complementary number in its absence. When two numbers are complementary, they work together to create harmony, and stability, or enhance certain traits in an individual.

9 is the complementary number for 1. It means if one is missing and 9 is present in your birth chart, then it can complement the absence of 1 in your birth chart.

5 and 7 are the complementary numbers for 2. If 2 is missing and 5 & 7 are present, then nothing to worry about. They may compensate for the absence of 2 to some extent.

Further, 5 & 7 can compensate for the number 3. In the absence of the number 3 in your birth chart, 5 & 7 if present can adjust to some extent.

Number 8 can compensate for the absence of 4. If number 4 does not find its place in your birth chart and 8 is present, then you may get some relief.

Who can compensate in the absence of number 5? Any idea about it? The answer is none, however, 6 can compensate marginally. **5 is a master key**

number and its presence in your birth chart is very important.

Number 5 can compensate for the absence of number 6. If 6 is missing from your birth chart and 5 is present, then nothing much to worry about.

Number 3 is the complementary number for 7. Can you remember 3, 5, and 7 form a horizontal line in the Lo-Shu Grid? 3 is knowledge and 7 is wisdom. Knowledge can compensate the wisdom to some extent.

8 is absent from your birth chart and 5 & 4 are present. Nothing to worry absence of 8 can be compensated by the presence of 5 & 4. 4 is a part of the vertical line commonly shared by 4 & 8.

As I have discussed 9 is the complementary number of 1. In the absence of 9 if 1 is present in your birth chart it can work for 9. Number 1 and number 9 are complementary to each other.

Now I feel you are a little bit relaxed. But still apprehensive about missing numbers, where no compensatory numbers are present. Be relaxed I am here to give you the best solutions for your excellence in life in the next chapters.

Conclusion:

The missing numbers in your numeroscope might initially seem daunting, but understanding the concept of complementary numbers brings a sense of balance and reassurance. Each number has a unique role in shaping your life. But, when one is absent, its complementary number can step in to fill the gap. This interconnectedness of numbers ensures that even if you're missing certain traits, there's often another number that can support you in achieving your goals.

As you move forward, keep in mind that your numeroscope is a guide—a tool to help you overcome life's challenges and opportunities with greater clarity. And remember, even if certain numbers are missing, there are always ways to enhance and balance your life's energy. Stay tuned, as the next chapters will offer you practical solutions and remedies to maximize your potential and create the life you desire.

Chapter four

REMEDIES FOR MISSING NUMBERS: EMPOWER YOURSELF WITH ELEMENTS

"Numerology is an ancient tool for unlocking the mysteries of the universe and discovering your life's purpose."

– Anonymous

I feel you all are familiar with the elements. Elements in nature refer to the fundamental substances that make up the physical world. In various cultures and philosophies, these elements are often categorized to represent the basic building blocks of life and the universe.

Do you know air, fire, wood, earth, sky, gold, and silver are called elements in various traditional systems? For example, in Indian philosophy sky, air, water, fire, and earth are five classical/physical elements. Our physical bodies are created out of the five elements. Greek philosophy considers air, water, fire, and earth as four classical elements. In Chinese traditional philosophy wood, fire, earth, metal, and water are included in five elements (Wu Xing). Silver and gold are often considered metals but in the alchemical tradition considered them as elements.

As we are part and parcel of the different elements and their imbalance creates problems for us, we can also use them for our betterment. The different elements can be used to redress the absence of missing numbers. Different numbers represent different elements.

4	9	2
WOOD	FIRE	EARTH
3	5	7
WOOD	EARTH	METAL SILVER
8	1	6
EARTH	WATER	METAL GOLDEN

Lo-Shu Grid

1→Water Element

2→ Earth Element

3→ Wood Element

4→Wood Element.

5→Earth Element.

6→Golden Metal

7→ Silver Metal

8→ Earth Element.

9→ Fire Element.

As 3 & 4 represent wood elements, we compensate for their absence from the birth chart with the use of wood elements. I hope you are now more excited to know what are the wood elements and how to use them for the benefit of individual people.

Wood Elements:

Rudrakshya (seeds of the Elaeocarpus ganitrus tree), Tulsi (Basil), Chandal(sandalwood), and any types of wood.

How to Use it?

Wear any rudrakshya (five-faced) mala, tulsi bead mala, or sandal mala around your neck. You may also wear a wooden bracelet around your wrist. For spiritual sanctity, the mala should consist of 108 beads.

2,5 & 8 form the diagonal line in the Lo-Shu grid is called the earth element. Using the earth elements, we may compensate for their absence from our birth chart.

Earth Elements:

Crystal is considered an earth element.

How to Use it?

Wear **a** crystal bracelet around your left wrist. You may also wear a crystal mala around your neck. You may also wear crystal even if with the presence of 2,5 and 8 numbers. Crystal can help you make clear decisions. Further, it can help, you include healing, meditation, and enhancing specific qualities or energies.

9 is a fire element. Fire means energy.

Fire Elements:

Red threads, red clothes.

How to Use it?

Wear red thread around your right wrist (in the case of male) and around your left arm (in case of female). Wear red clothes, and keep a handkerchief of red color with you. Clean the threads regularly.

1 is a water element.

Water Element: Water

How to Use it?

- Drink sufficient water. If you are drinking 2 liters of water daily, increase it to 2.5 to 3 liters.

- Offer water to the sun before 7 AM daily. You may ask how to offer water to the sun? is there any prescribed method? Yes, there is a prescribed way of offering water. Take a round-necked small copper vessel, tie a red thread around its neck, put red vermilion, sunned rice, and sugar/ jaggery in the water, and offer the sun. After bathing take the vessel up to your neck height and drop the water constantly looking at the sun. The shadow of the falling water must fall on your body. Take care to collect the offering water in a bucket to water the plant.

Number 7 represents silver metal.

How to Use it?

Wear a metal strap wristwatch of golden and silver mixed color.

Number 6 represents the golden metal. But remember 6 represents white color.

How to Use it?

Wear a metal strap wristwatch of golden color. The dial of the watch must be reasonably bigger with the 1 to 12 marking. The number indicating 6 must be visible clearly without any cut.

These are very simple and inexpensive methods that can enhance your success and boost your confidence. Have faith in yourself and in your belief system.

Conclusion:

The remedies for missing numbers offer a practical way to restore balance and harmony in your life by harnessing the power of the elements. Each element—whether it's wood, earth, fire, water, or metal—holds a unique energy that can fill the gaps left by missing numbers in your numeroscope. By incorporating these elements into your daily routine, such as wearing a rudraksha mala, crystal bracelet, or even something as simple as drinking more water, you can align yourself with the natural forces that govern the universe.

These remedies are not just symbolic; they are tools that can empower you to overcome obstacles, enhance your strengths, and bring a sense of completeness to your life. Remember, the journey to personal growth is about taking small, meaningful steps every day. Embrace these practices with faith and confidence, knowing that you are actively working to create a more balanced and successful life. Now, let's move forward to the next chapter, where more insights and solutions await.

Chapter five

REMEDIES FOR MISSING NUMBERS: A MASTERSTROKE

"The numbers are a guide, not a guarantee. They open doors to understanding and insight, but it is up to you to walk through them."

– Anonymous

Have you heard about Yantra? You may or may not heard about it. But it is a very popular concept in easter philosophy.

Yantra derives its name from *"yan"* which means control, curb, or influence, and *"tra"* which means Tool. It is a tool or diagram illustrating sacred geometric order that emits sacred cosmic positive energy and eliminates negative energy. As you know everything is connected with energy.

Negative energy may foil your plans whereas positive energy can give you abundance in life.

A yantra is hugely used in Hindu and Buddhist spiritual practices. It is the body of the divine God or Goddess in symbolic form. The yantra originated primarily in tantric traditions in Eastern philosophy to get the ultimate truth in life. Tantric philosophy emphasizes the potential for spiritual liberation within the physical world. Yantras are used as tools for harnessing and transforming energy. The practitioners of tantra believed that cosmic energy (Shakti) is directed toward the practitioner. When Yantra is energized by the mantra in tantric practice evolved. Furthermore, in many Hindu rituals yantras are used regularly and worshipped by mantra.

For example, **Laxmi Yantra** which is otherwise called Lo-Shu Grid in numerology. In Hindu Mythology Laxmi Yantra is considered sacred and represents the goddess of wealth and prosperity Laxmi.

4	9	2
3	5	7
8	1	6

Yantra is often composed of various shapes, such as triangles, circles, and floral patterns, representing different gods or goddesses. Gods and goddesses are the sources of divine or cosmic energy. In Yantra, different numbers and designs are made for specific purposes. Yantras are used as tools for meditation, concentration, to achieve specific goals, and to achieve spiritual goals. They are believed to have mystical powers and can be found in temples, homes, and spiritual texts throughout South Asia.

The use of Yantra can be a game-changer in numerology. It can enhance the energy level of the missing numbers and balance the chart for empowerment. **Yanta is used as a direct remedy** for the deficits in a birth chart. In numerological remedies, 8 yantras are widely used to be fitted in any date of birth.

1. Surya-Budh Yantra

2. Sun -Pyra Yantra

3. Budh-Pyra Yantra

4. Pyra Yantra

5. Surya Yantra

6. Budh Yantra

7. Gayatri Yantra

8. Saraswati Yantra

Yantra can be encrypted with brass, silver, gold, copper, etc. Further, Bhuj Patra (Birch Bark), and paper are used for making yantras for different purposes. But for use in numerology to enhance the power of different numbers different yantras are made in silver or copper in triangular or round-shaped pendants.

In the Surya Budha Yantra pendant one side contains Surya Yantra and another side contains Budha Yantra. Mostly silver metal is used for a better look and benefits.

Are you eager to know what is written or encrypted on Surya and Budha Yantra? Now see what is there.

Surya Yantra

6	1	8
7	5	3
2	9	4

Budh-Yantra

9	4	11
10	8	6
5	12	7

Pyra Yantra (Laxmi Yantra/ Lo-Shu Grid)

4	9	2
3	5	7
8	1	6

1.

Surya -Budha Yantra:

It is a triangular shape pendant with Surya Yantra on one side and Budha Yantra on the other side comes with red and green threads to wear around the neck.

Who can wear it?

Surya Yantra is used to uplift the MOOLANKA- -BHAGYANKA in the birth chart.

Budh Yantra is used when 5 is missing and 6 is present in the birth chart. **But care should be taken that** MOOLANKA or BHAGYANKA **should not be 8. Why? Because this is a direct remedy 1 and 8 are anti planets and non-friends.**

Example,

4	9	2
3		7
	1	6

M-2 B-4

In this instance case Surya-Budh Yantra can be used. Here both 2 and 4 are non-friends. Surya can uplift the M & B whereas Budha can fulfill the missing number 5.

2.

Surya-Pyra Yantra

This Surya yantra is used to uplift M & B when 5 is present and 6 is missing from the birth chart. Pyra will take care of the missing number 6 along with other missing numbers. But there are conditions as such;

- The MOOLANKA or BHAGYANKA should not be 8.
- The MOOLANKA or BHAGYANKA should not be 3.

Why such a condition?

Because 8 is anti of 1 and the same principle is applied to 3 & 6.

Example,

4	9	2
	5	7
8	1	

M-4 B-9

In this instance case, Surya Yantra can uplift M and B, and Pyra can fulfill the missing number 6 and uplift other numbers.

3.

Budh-Pyra Yantra

This yantra can be used when both 5 and 6 numbers are missing from the birth chart. Provided the MOOLANKA or BHAGYANKA is not 3. You may ask why. Because 3 and 6 are anti-planet. Direct remedies can't be made for 6 if the MOOLANKA or BHAGYANKA number is 3.

For example,

	999	22
8	11	

M-1 B-2

4.

Pyra yantra

Pyra yantra can be used when the number 6 is missing and 5 is present in the birth chart. Provided that

- the MOOLANKA or BHAGYANKA is 8

- the MOOLANKA or BHAGYANKA should not be 3.

For example,

4	9	2
	5	
8	1	

M-8 B-4

5.

Surya Yantra

We can use Surya Yantra when the MOOLANKA-BHAGYANKA combination is either 3-6 or 6-3 and 5 is present. Remember both 6-3 are antiplanets and we can't do the remedies of either 3 or 6, for which to uplift the chart Surya Yantra can be beneficial.

For example,

	99	
3	5	
	1	6

M-3, B-6

6.

Budh yantra

We can use Budh Yantra when the number 5 is missing. Provided that the MOOLANKA and BHAGYANKA number are 3-8 or 8-3. Number 6 may be present or absent.

For example,

4	9	2
3		
8	1	

M-3, B-8

Budha Yantra can compensate for the missing number 5 and uplift other numbers. As 5 keeps the center position it keeps balance in the chart. In this instance, cases 2, 5, and 8 create a Raja Yoga after Budha Yantra is used.

7.

Gayatri Yantra

In Hindu religion and philosophy, Gayatri Mantra is very auspicious. It is sacred and has spiritual significance. It is a Vedic mantra that has many positive impacts on our minds and souls if recited in a prescribed manner.

Likely the Gayatri Yantra is based on intricate geometric patterns, often including triangles, circles, and squares. On the one side the Gayatri Mantra is inscribed on the yantra and other side Depictions of Goddess Gayatri with five heads are common. The Gayatri yantra is energized with Vedic rituals after its creation. To wear the Yantra, its pendulum or locket form is better. Gayatri yantra made of silver is better for use.

Why use for?

When you find a person very sick. Despite good treatment not recovering as expected. Prescribe this wonderful yantra to wear around his neck and see the magic. You may advise him to recite the Gayatri mantra in mind for a speedy recovery.

Irrespective of any MOOLANKA or BHAGYANKA number you can use Gayatri Yantra.

8.

Saraswati Yantra

One side of the yantra often depicts Goddess Saraswati with four arms, holding a veena, a book, a rosary, and a lotus, and the other side is composed of intricate geometric shapes, including triangles, circles, and squares, which symbolize different aspects of the goddess's energy.

It can be made from various materials, including copper, brass, gold, silver, or paper.

The size of the yantra may vary widely, from small pendants to large wall hangings. For wearing around the neck, a pendant is a good option.

Why use for?

Parents are often worried about the education of their children. Some parents complain that their children are not able to concentrate on their studies and not getting any improvement on their journey. The children are expressing their unhappiness with schooling and so on. If these are the problems then Saraswati Yantra is a better solution.

Benefits of Using a Saraswati Yantra

- Enhance the intellect and wisdom of your child.

- Improve the concentration and memory of your kids.

- Increase the creativity and artistic abilities of your kids.

- Success in education and examinations will glorify you.

- Overall spiritual growth

You can use the Saraswati Yantra provided that no MOOLANKA or BHAGYANKA number is 6.

When to wear Yantra?

When to wear the yantra is very important. Specific time has been prescribed.

- The time should be Sukla Paksha. (Sukla Paksha is a Sanskrit term that refers to the bright fortnight or the waxing phase of the moon in the Hindu calendar. It's a period of 15 days that begins after the Amavasya (new moon) and culminates on Purnima (full moon).

  Shukla Paksha is generally considered an auspicious time for starting new ventures, performing rituals, and undertaking important tasks. It is believed to be a period of both spiritual and material growth.

- Date should not be 4 or 8. (4 and 8 are not considered auspicious in numerology as Rahu and Saturn are slow planets)

- No Rahu Kaal (Rahu Kaal is a specific period of each day considered inauspicious in Hindu astrology. It's believed to be influenced by the planet Rahu, a shadow planet with a **malefic nature**.

  The duration of Rahu kaal is approximately 90 minutes each day. Timing of the period may vary based on location and date. It's generally avoided for starting new ventures, important decisions, or auspicious activities.)

- The day must not be Saturday.

- Should wear with specified colored threads.

Name of Yantra	Color of the Threads
Surya -Budh	Red+ Green
Surya-Pyra	Red+ White
Budh-Pyra	Green + White
Pyra	White
Surya	Red
Budh	Green
Gayatri	Yellow
Saraswati	Yellow

The thread length must be sufficient so that the yantra can touch the Anahat/Hrudaya chakra (heart chakra). The silver material of the yantra may turn black over time and must be cleaned with toothpaste or tamarind. If you use Yantra with a copper material must be cleaned with tamarind.

The use of yantras is the direct remedy for missing numbers and uplifting of MOOLANKA and BHAGYANKA. While selecting yantras for a specific birth chart proper studies on missing numbers, MOOLANKA, and BHAGYANKA be made.

Conclusion:

Yantras provides a powerful and ancient remedy for balancing and uplifting the energies in your numerology chart. These sacred geometric tools are more than just symbols; they are conduits of cosmic energy, designed to enhance your strengths and address the missing elements in your birth chart. Whether it's the Surya-Budh Yantra to uplift your core numbers or the Saraswati Yantra to boost intellectual growth, each serves a unique purpose tailored to your needs.

The use of Yantras is not just about correcting numerical imbalances—it's about connecting with the deeper, mystical forces of the universe. By wearing these Yantras, energized with mantras and crafted in materials like silver or copper, you align yourself with the divine energies that can transform your life. The careful selection of Yantras based on your MOOLANKA, BHAGYANKA, and the specific numbers in your chart ensures that you are receiving the most potent form of spiritual support.

As you incorporate these Yantras into your life, remember to honor the rituals associated with them, such as wearing them during auspicious times and keeping them clean and energized. These small acts of reverence amplify their power, bringing you closer to your goals and spiritual fulfillment.

With the right Yantra, you're not just filling in the gaps in your numerology chart—you're taking a masterstroke toward a more balanced, prosperous, and enlightened life. Now, let's move into the next chapter to continue this journey of self-discovery and empowerment.

Chapter six

REMEDIES FOR MISSING NUMBERS: NATURAL REMEDIES

"Numbers have a way of taking a man by the hand and leading him down the path of reason."

– Pythagoras

This is the third remedy for the upliftment of date of birth. These types of remedies include every number, missing numbers as well as numbers present in the chart. These natural and inexpensive remedies must be included in your daily routine as a habit. Now let us go through the remedies for each number.

1

SUN

The Sun is the king of the solar system and the birth chart. If the sun is weak in your birth chart you may not be able to communicate your thoughts, in a clear, smart, and articulated manner. You may lose confidence during any discussions and may be "speech-impaired. Choosing a profession may be an issue.

Actionable steps;

- ✓ Rise early before sunrise and be exposed to sunray.

- ✓ After you wake up in the morning see yourself in the mirror for about 2 minutes.

- ✓ Touch the feet of your parent in the morning. In their absence, you may salute the photographs of your parents.

- ✓ Have a bath putting rose petals in the water.

- ✓ Safeguard the government property.

- ✓ Offer water to the sun before 7 AM every day. You may ask how to offer water to the Sun? Is there any prescribed method? Yes, there is a prescribed way of offering water. Take a round-necked small copper vessel, tie a red thread around its neck, put red vermilion, sunned rice/"raw rice" (akshyat), and sugar/ jaggery in the water, and offer the sun. After bathing take the vessel up to your neck height and drop the water constantly looking at the sun. The shadow of the falling water must fall on your body. Take care to collect the offering water in a bucket to water the plant. Care must be taken that the offering water must not drop on your legs.

(If you are governed by 8(Moolanka or Bhagyanka) no steps, be taken to appease Sun)

2

MOON

Moon is the queen. It represents sensitivity and intuitions. It regulates our minds. For clarity in judgment and mood, uplifting the moon is necessary.

Actionable steps;

- Offer water, green coconut water, milk, milk plus water, and Panchamrit (Panchamrit is a traditional mixture used in Hindu rituals and ceremonies. The word "Panchamrit" is derived from Sanskrit, where *"Pancha"* means five and *"amrita"* means nectar. Thus, Panchamrit is considered to be a nectar made from five ingredients. These ingredients typically include Milk, curd, honey, jaggery, and ghee) to shiva to appease. One name of Shiva is Chandrashekhar because he bears the moon at his head.

- You can sit under the moonlight. If married both the couple should enjoy moonlight for a better future.

- Worship the moon on 2nd day of Sukla Pakshya (2nd day of the moon's waxing phase). You may ask how to worship the moon. Make a small full moon in silver. Keep it in a pot and worship with white flowers, sunned rice, "Durva," "Darbha," or "Bermuda grass,"

3

JUPITER

Jupiter is the Guru or the mentor of Gods. He is the symbol of knowledge, imagination, and creativity. To appease Jupiter and enhance his strength in your birth chart you need to uplift number 3.

Actionable steps;

> ➢ Do saffron tilak on your forehead after a bath every day. Do it at the back side of your tongue, and naval point also.

> ➢ Every Thurs day, water the banana plant and offer jaggery and gram dal. Never forget to offer a ghee lamp to the plant. Remember that the worship of the banana plant should not be made on your own campus. It should be at any public place like a park or temple.

> **(If you are governed by 6(Moolanka or Bhagyanka) no steps, be taken to appease Jupiter)**

4

RAHU

Rahu is a symbol of discipline and organization. No one can do well in life without discipline in self, workspace, society, etc. Similarly, acting in an organized way for a better cause is beneficial for society. Appease Rahu is necessary for self-discipline and organization.

Actionable steps;

Feed dogs or crows pieces of bread soaked with milk. It may be better to feed them daily. If not possible, do it once or twice a week outside your campus.

5

MERCURY

Mercury creates balance in life. Do you remember its place in the Lo-Shu Grid? It is positioned at the center of the chart with an equal distance from every digit. To achieve continuous success in personal and professional life, upliftment of number 5 is necessary.

Actionable steps;

- ➢ Free the parrot (green-colored bird) from the cage. On Wednesday buy a parrot, take it home, serve the bird for two to three days, and free it opening the cage. You can do this practice once in three months.

- ➢ Use more and more green colors in your life. For example, wear green clothes, use green color pens, and handkerchiefs, eat green vegetables, walk in the park, and enjoy nature under green trees.

6

VENUS

Venus is a symbol of relationships, family bonding, luxury, and happiness. Imagine a family without love and affection. No good relationships between a couple, and their children. No peace in the family but chaos. The very family structure is disturbed. The absence, or a weak Venus can do all the above issues making life difficult.

Actionable steps;

Donate white things like milk, sugar, barfi, rasgulla, etc. to physically challenged persons on Friday. If such persons are not available you may give such things to beggars. Because Venus is considered disabled and has lost one eye during Vaman incarnation of lord Vishnu.

(If you are governed by 3(Moolanka or Bhagyanka) no steps, be taken to appease Venus)

7

KETU

Ketu is lower part of Rahu. Number 7 is a symbol of wisdom, education, spiritualism, music, dance, drama, and creative awareness.

Actionable steps;

As prescribed for number 4. Feed dogs or crows pieces of bread soaked with milk. It may be better to feed them daily. If not possible, do it once or twice a week outside your campus.

8

SATURN

Number 8 is a symbol of money and finance. Do you imagine a life without money and financial security, A hopeless situation? Nobody needs it. Uplifting of 8 is necessary for all.

Actionable steps;

- Visit the Shani temple on Saturday and read the Shani Chalisa.

- Offer mustard oil, black cloth, and black gram in the temple or donate to poor people.

- Donate some coins to sweepers preferably on Saturday.

- Do the shoe service in Gurudwar or temple.

- Never involved in arguments with lower cast/class people.

- Eat vegetarian foods on Saturday.

- Never apply oil on your body on Saturday.

  (If you are governed by 1(Moolanka or Bhagyanka) no steps, be taken to appease Saturn)

9

MARS

Mars is a symbol of memory, respect, and resilience. It enhances self-esteem and respect for others. How can you succeed in life without sharp memory and self-respect? Without respecting others, you may not get respect. Remember all the behaviors are reciprocal. As you sow, sow you reap. It is the universal truth.

Actionable steps;

- ✓ Read Hanuman Chalisa every day, and preferably on Tuesday.

- ✓ Read Bajrang Ban or listen to it.

- ✓ Offer jasmine oil and sindoor/vermilion to Hanuman on Tuesday.

<u>**Remedies are required for which numbers?**</u>

For the MOOLANKA, BHAGYANKA, and missing numbers. But for anti D-C no remedies be made. Remedies be made for opposite D-C.

Examples

1

4	9	22
3		7
	11	66

M-4, B-2, K-6

Remedies for 4, 2, and 5 be made. Why? 4 and 2 are opposite numbers and 5 is a missing number. Why remedies for 8 is not made? Because 2 and 8 are anti-numbers. No direct remedies for anti-numbers are advised.

2

	9	2
3		7
8	1	6

M-1, B-8, K-6

In this case, remedies for 5, 6, 4, and 7 be made. No remedies for 1, 8, and 3. Why? Because 1 and 8 are anti-numbers. As remedies made for 6 no remedies for 3 as 3 and 6 are anti-numbers.

3

4	9	2
3		
	1	6

M-3, B-6, K-1

Remedies for 1, 4, 2, and 7 be made. No remedies for 3 and 6 are recommended as both are anti planets.

4

	999	
	5	7
8	111	6

M-1, B-7 K-5

Remedies for all the numbers are recommended except 6 and 8. Because 6 is anti to 3 and 8 is anti to 1.

5

4	9	22
	5	
8	1	

M-8 B-4 K-2

Remedies for 8,4,9,5, and 6 be made. No remedies for 3 and 8 are recommended. Because 1 is anti to 8 and 6 is anti to 3.

All the above remedies work if followed regularly.

Conclusion:

Numbers, in their essence, are more than mere digits; they are the fundamental forces guiding our lives. As Pythagoras aptly said, numbers lead us down the path of reason, showing us how to align ourselves with the cosmic energies they represent. But understanding these numbers isn't just about knowing your strengths—it's also about recognizing your weaknesses, especially when certain numbers are missing or imbalanced in your birth chart.

Natural remedies provide a practical and accessible way to address these imbalances. By incorporating these simple, yet powerful, actions into your daily routine, you can harness the energy of the numbers and bring harmony into your life. From the rising sun's first rays to the serene moonlight, from the warmth of saffron on your forehead to the offering of jasmine oil to Hanuman, these remedies are grounded in centuries-old wisdom.

The remedies for each number are not merely rituals; they are daily habits that nurture your mind, body, and spirit. Whether it's feeding crows and dogs to appease Rahu and Ketu, or offering water to the Sun to boost your confidence, these actions serve as subtle yet potent tools to transform your life. They bring balance where there is an imbalance, clarity where there is confusion, and strength where there is weakness.

However, it's important to remember that while these remedies can uplift your MOOLANKA, BHAGYANKA, and other critical numbers, they should be approached with care and understanding. Anti-numbers, for example, require a different strategy; not all numbers should be directly remedied.

Incorporating these natural remedies into your life is more than just a practice—it's a commitment to self-improvement and spiritual growth. By doing so, you align yourself with the universal energies, inviting prosperity, wisdom, and peace into your life. As you continue on this journey, let these numbers guide you, and may you find the balance and harmony you seek.

Chapter seven

NAME SPELLING CORRECTION: A NEW DIMENSION FOR YOUR LIFE.

"Numerology is the bridge between who you are now and who you have the potential to be."

– Anonymous

Everyone is identified by a name. The name gives you identity, fame, and success. Your name becomes a brand.

"Your brand is what people say about you when you're not in the room." - Jeff Bezos.

Do you believe it or not? The great people on this earth have brand values. Great people mean a name. A name is a brand.

For example, Mahatma Gandhi, a brand of nonviolence and peace. Abraham Lincoln was a brand of humanism and emancipator of bonded labor. Tesla a brand of motor vehicle. Space X, NASA, ISRO, Facebook, alphabet, Reliance Industries, Saudi Aramco, etc. are the names that represent different brands of products.

Now we see like humans, our pets have names including different companies that produce different products for our consumption. Every place, river, mountain, plant, creeper, animal, bird, vehicle, temple, mosque, church, educational institution, star, planet, etc. is identified by a name. Why do we name all the objects on this earth and universe? Because a name is a symbol of identity. A mark of empowering thoughts. We have named everything for our understanding and a better appreciation.

But do you know the name spelling of a person or a company or a product can make you or break you?

Have you ever thought about the correct spelling of a product name can skyrocket its demand? The reverse is also true. The correct answer is numerology.

In numerology, name spelling is associated with the practice of Chaldean and Pythagorean numerology systems. These systems assign numerical values to letters in the alphabet, which are then used to calculate various numbers associated with a person's name.

Chaldean ancient system assigns numbers to letters based on the sound vibration of each letter. This system is known for its focus on the energy and vibration of the name and is considered more mystical and esoteric.

Pythagorean Numerology is named after the Greek philosopher Pythagoras, which is more widely used and assigns numbers to letters in a straightforward, sequential manner (A=1, B=2, C=3, etc.). The Pythagorean system is more structured and is commonly used for analyzing names and birthdates. The maximum value of an alphabet is 8 and the minimum value is 1. Number 9 is not allotted to any number.

The alphabet with numerical values is as follows;

Number	1	2	3	4	5	6	7	8
	A	B	C	D	E	U	O	F
	I	K	G	M	H	V	Z	P
	J	R	L	T	N	W		
	Q		S		X			
	Y							

Now we got the value of all the alphabets from A to Z as above.

Are you excited to know how to and what to correct your name? How to know that your name spelling is correct or have to do something to correct it for a better result and success? Honestly speaking all we need is success in our lives, but despite our best efforts and sincerity we often fail. Why?

Numerology says correct name spelling can enhance your performance by 40 percent. Are you astonished? It is natural to be astonished when someone comes to encounter a new reality.

Now come to the real amazing journey. In numerology 1, 5, 6, and 3 are considered lucky, auspicious, and special. The total numerical value of any name spelling should come to any of the one-number after analyzing the birth chart.

When the name spelling should come to 1?

The first option is 1. Number 1 represents the Sun, the king of the numeroscope. It is a number of successes and authority. Your name spelling should come to one when both 5 and 6 numbers are present in your birth chart. Provided that MOOLANKA or BHAGYANK is not 8. Why not 8? Because 8 is a nonfriend of the Sun.

When the name spelling should come to 5?

Correction of name spelling is a way to uplift your birth chart. Spelling correction should come to 5, on the following conditions.

- When 5 is missing from the birth chart.

- Diagonal line 2, 5 & 8 or 4,5 & 6 or both the lines are completed.

When the name spelling should come to **6**?

Number 6 is a symbol of relationships, family bonding, luxury, and happiness. Name spelling should come to 6 provided that;

- ✓ 6 is missing from the birth chart.

- ✓ The diagonal line consisting of 4,5 & 6 is going to be completed.

- ✓ MOOLANKA or BHAGYANK is not 3.

When the name spelling should come to **3**?

This is the 4th option before you bring your name spelling to 3. The conditions are as follows;

- ✓ If number 3 is missing from the chart.

- ✓ Neither your MOOLANKA nor BHAGYANK is 6.

- ✓ If you are in a Jupiter-related profession.

SOME BEST SPELLING OF COMPANY AND PRODUCTS.

DLF. The value of the letters comes to D (4) +L (3) +F (8) =15=1+5=6

DLF is an Indian commercial real estate company founded in 1946 based in New Delhi. It is a very successful commercial establishment with revenue touching ₹ 6,958 (US $ 830 million) in 2024 with net income coming to ₹ 2724(US $ 330 million) and the total assets of the company a whopping ₹60,262(US $ 7.2 billion) in 2024. The credit goes to DLF name spelling.

ALTO is a premier brand name for a household car in India manufactured by Maruti Suzuki. As of 2024, the company has sold over 5 million units in India since 2006. The spelling of the ALTO comes to A (1) +L (3) +T (4) +O (7) =15=6

INDICA is the familiar brand of TATA motors in India launched on 30 December 1998. The annual sale of the car was as high as 1,44,690 units in 2006-2007. As of July 2009, the average monthly sales of Indica were 8000 units. The said models were exported to Europe and African countries from late 2004. The said model was discontinued in April 2018. The spelling of INDICA comes to 1+5+4+1+3+1=15=6

TATA's brand value now comes to $28.6 billion, according to the latest Brand Finance India 100 2014 report. It is India's most valuable brand. What is the total number of TATA? 4+1+4+1=10=1. Yes, it comes to 1.

PARLE -G was the first FMCG product to cross ₹ 5000 crore mark in India in 2013. Parle is the No. 1 biscuit company in the world started its production in India in the year 1929. Now calculate the numerical value of Parle. 8+1+2+3+5=19=1. It comes to 1.

Reliance Industries Limited is a Fortune 500 company and the largest private-sector corporation in India with a brand value of ₹ 65,320 crore. The numerical value of Reliance Industries Limited comes to 2+5+3+1+5+5+3+5=28=10=1

1+5+4+6+3+4+2+1+5+3=34=7
3+1+4+1+4+5+4=22=4

The value of the first name comes to 1 and the total value of the entire company comes to 3.

NASA- NASA is the world's best space organization and achieved hundreds of path-breaking research and discoveries in space science. The total numerical values of NASA come to 5+1+3+1=10=1. 1 represents the sun, which means energy, that is why NASA is so successful in space science on this planet. The abbreviation of NASA is The(4+5+5=14=5)   National (5+1+4+1+7+5+1+3=27=9)   Aeronautic (1+5+2+7+5+1+6+4+1+3+3=38=11=2)   and (1+5+4=10=1)   Space(3+8+1+3+5) Administration(1+4+4+1+5+1+3+4+2+1+4+1+7+ 5=43=8) now if we add all the numerical values of an abbreviated form of NASA we got 5+9+2+1+8=25=7 Now 7 represents Ketu that means wisdom and directs toward research and giving new dimensions to our knowledge. NASA is doing the same thing in space science.

MRF is an Indian multinational tyre company and the largest manufacturer of tyres in India founded in 1946. MRF was named the world's second strongest tyre brand by brand finance, with an AAA-brand grade. The numerical value of MRF comes to (4+2+8) =14=5

Ratan Tata (21415 4141) =5. The complete name is Ratan Naval Tata (21415 51613 4141=3) Both the name spellings suit the Indian industrialist and philanthropist as his MOOKANKA is 1.

How do you write correct spelling?

For example,

Raj (2 1 1) Kumar (2 6 4 1 2) Seth (3 5 4 5) =9

First name spelling should not come to 4 or 8. Now, the correct spelling should be RAAJ KUMAR SETH, as the total number of the name comes to 1. You may write the above name as R K SETH (2 2 3 5 4 5=21=3) but you should not write as R.K.Seth. When a dot is given the force is diluted in the name spelling. If R K Seth is a doctor, how can he write a doctor in his name? It is very simple just write Dr. R K Seth or Dr. RAAJ KUMAR SETH.

But, remember the best name spelling is only possible as per your date of birth, where the secrets of your success are hiding.

How to write the company name?

When we chose a company name that is near to our heart. But most of us never think about its correct spelling, its effects on the success of the company, and future growth and prospects. Even a coma, full stops, space, and bracket may break the energy flow of the name spelling including the line.

For example,

1. Sciencetec. Limited.

2. Sciencetec Company. Ltd

3. Sciencetec Company. Limited.

4. Sciencetec (Company) Limited.

5. Sciencetec

   Company Limited.

6. Sciencetec Company (Pvt) Limited.

Now if we verify the numerical value of Sciencetec it comes to 3315535455=39=12=3. Similarly, the numerical value of the word **company** comes to 3748151=29=11=2. Number 3 is for Sciencetec and 5 for Sciencetec Company.

All the above spelling for the company is correct if written in the above format. Your name spelling and company name spelling should be compatible with each other. For example, if your name spelling comes to 1, then your company and product names should come to 5, 6, or 3, which can increase the success rate.

Product name examples,

SHAKTI=5

PEARL=1

RINO=6

SURF=1

HOW TO IMPLEMENT THE NAME SPELLING CORRECTION WITHOUT CHANGING YOUR OFFICIAL DOCUMENTS?

Are you excited to implement the corrected name spelling without changing official documents? Am I right? You can use the corrected name in the following items or ways.

- Visiting card-It has no binding on your official document.

- Mail id-example; akkkanda9@gmail.com, rksharma99@gmail.com

- Social media accounts, such as Facebook, X, Instagram, Linkedin, Telegram, etc.

- Nameplate- It is your freedom to write your lucky spelling.

- Website -Example, arunkumarrk.com

Conclusion:

The power of a name goes far beyond mere identification; it's a vital part of your personal and professional success. By understanding and aligning your name's spelling with numerological principles, you can tap into a new level of potential and achievement.

Names like DLF, ALTO, and NASA show how the right name can lead to tremendous success. Similarly, correcting your name to match favorable numerological numbers—such as 1, 5, 6, or 3—can positively influence your life and career.

You don't need to make official changes to experience these benefits. Simple adjustments like updating your visiting cards, email addresses, and social media profiles can bring you closer to your goals.

Acknowledge the energy level and power of your name. By doing so, you're not just enhancing your identity; you're setting the stage for a more successful and fulfilling life.

Chapter eight

LOVE MARRIAGE OR ARRANGED MARRIAGE

"A Hindu wedding is a vibrant and joyous celebration of love, filled with rituals and customs that have been passed down through generations."

– Unknown

n Indian society, marriage is considered a sacrament. Throughout human life, three important ceremonies are observed such as birth rituals, marriage ceremonies, and death rituals. When family and friends observe the birth rituals of a newborn, he can't enjoy or understand them. Similarly, the death rituals left the family and friends to mourn and memories his contributions to his family and society without his physical presence. Now the only ceremony left for the person is marriage which he can enjoy. In Indian society when we think about the marriage of a son or daughter it always reminds us of the arranged marriage with the consent of both the families bride and groom. With time, the concept of marriage is changing, and the concept of love marriage is gaining ground in our society. However, marriage is taken very seriously as it is associated with the value system, morality, and cultural backing of our society.

Do you think numerology or astrology has some clue to conclude which kind of marriage is possible for the person? If you believe the planets are present in our universe and they influence our understanding of our universe and thinking process, then it is a fact that we can forecast the type of marriage for a person without any doubt.

In numerology 5,6 & 7 numbers play a crucial role in a marriage. From the birth chart, we can forecast an arranged or love marriage and its stability.

Love marriage

Example of a scenario,

		2
	5	77
	1	6

M-1 B-6

In the above birth chart,

- Love marriage is possible with its stability, as 77 and 6 are present.
- When only 77 are present and 6 are absent then a love marriage will happen without its stability.
- When 77 and 5 are present then a love marriage will happen with a 50% chance of survival.
- If 777 is present love marriage is possible but without the presence of 5 or 6 the marriage mayn't survive.

As you know 5 makes balance in life and has no nonfriends in the chart and 6 represents family, glamor, party, enjoyment, sexual pleasure, etc. 7 is wisdom and it thinks from the heart not from the brain. Ketu can be exploited emotionally so it can go for love and marriage without future planning or consequences. The presence of 6 can give guidance to 7 as 7 is the disciple of 6 (Venus).

Arranged marriage

Example of a scenario;

	9	22
33		
		6

M-3 B-3

In the above chart, no love marriage but arranged marriage is a possibility. Why such a prediction? You can ask further. Because,

- Presence of 3(Jupiter) and 9(mars) in the chart are against love marriage.
- Multiple 33 and 6 present calls for an arranged marriage.
- If MOOLANKA-BHAGYANKA are 2,3,9 symbolizes arranged marriage.

However, the past life experiences of different incarnations and karmic accounts make a difference in shaping people's lives.

Conclusion:

When it comes to the question of love marriage versus arranged marriage, the perspective is deeply rooted in individual and cultural values. In Indian society, both types of marriages are seen as significant, each with its own set of traditions and expectations.

Numerology offers an intriguing lens through which we can explore these marital paths. By analyzing numbers in your birth chart, we can gain insights into the likelihood of a love marriage or an arranged one, and how stable that marriage might be.

For those who find 5, 6, and 7 prominently featured in their charts, love marriages often appear as a viable and potentially stable option. However, the presence of these numbers alone doesn't guarantee success. Your mindset and family influences can play crucial roles.

On the other hand, a chart dominated by 3, 9, and multiple instances of 33 suggests that arranged marriages are more likely. These numbers align more closely with traditional values and stability in marital arrangements.

Ultimately, while numerology can provide guidance, the choice between love and arranged marriage is deeply personal. It is further influenced by many factors, including past experiences and individual preferences. Whether you are drawn to the romance of a love marriage or the stability of an arranged one, what matters most is the mutual respect, understanding, and commitment you bring to the relationship.

Chapter nine

THE MAGIC OF THE COMBINATIONS OF NUMBERS

"Numbers are the Universal language offered by the deity to humans as confirmation of the truth."

– St. Augustine

Loshu Grid has nine blocks containing 3 vertical, 3 horizontal, and 2 diagonal lines. Each block contains a specific number and is arranged so beautifully that the total of each line comes to 15.

First, let me show you the grid for a better understanding of the grid and numbers.

4	9	2
3	5	7
8	1	6

HORIZONTAL LINES OR PLANES

4 RAHU	9 MARS	2 MOON

Now we see 4, 9, and 2 constitute the first horizontal line, where 4 represents Rahu, 9 represents Mars and 2 represents the Moon. This line is called **MENTAL PLANE**. Then what does it indicate? If all three numbers are present in a numeroscope, indicates that the person is brilliant a god-gifted brain. Can remember things easily without much effort.

He is mentally very strong and can do something unique. Do you learn something from the first horizontal line? What is the message for us? The message is planets like Rahu, Mars, and Moon create a Yoga in the birth chart making the person brilliant and sharp-minded.

3 JUPITER	5 MERCURY	7 KETU

Now see the second horizontal line formed taking 3,5 and 7 numbers. This particular line is called **EMOTIONAL OR SOUL PLANE.** The people having such lines are God-loving, spiritual, compassionate, very emotional, and sentimental. They are very soft-hearted. They can't see the sufferings of others. They are much more likely to be moved by the emotional appeals of others. They are very trusted people and trust others easily. For this type of tendency, they are often cheated by others in their lives. They easily be fooled by others.

The tagline for these types of people is "they are people of golden heart. The heart rules not the head. You can trust them blindly without a second thought."

8 **SATURN**	1 **SUN**	6 **VENUS**

The third horizontal line is formed containing 8, 1, and 6. This line is called **PRACTICAL PLANE. It is also a line of prosperity.** People having this line in their numeroscope are very practical in their approach to actions and logical-minded.

They possess an analytical brain. They don't believe anyone easily. You can't convince them easily or win their hearts. They are not to be emotionally exploited. You may not win them logically. They try to apply logic to everything for which they are misunderstood sometimes.

VERTICAL PLANES

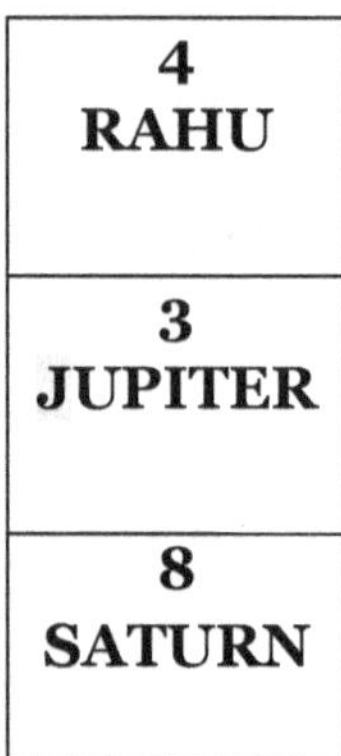

Let me talk about the vertical plane. The first vertical line contains 4,3 and 8 numbers. This line is called **THOUGHT PLANE**. If a numeroscope has this vertical line complete, it is presumed that the person is a thinker. His thought process is very strong. He is a very farsighted man. He can judge the market sentiment in advance. He can anticipate profit or loss in business in the future. His actions are based on well-articulated thought and reasoning. They can take a calculated risk. For example, he can buy a property for 10 lakhs for now eyeing for 1 crore after ten years, which can't be anticipated by a common man. After 10 years he can get the amount more or less than one crore. In fact, they are disciplined, well-organized, cunning, well-planned, and can visualize things better. This plane can suit best for politics.

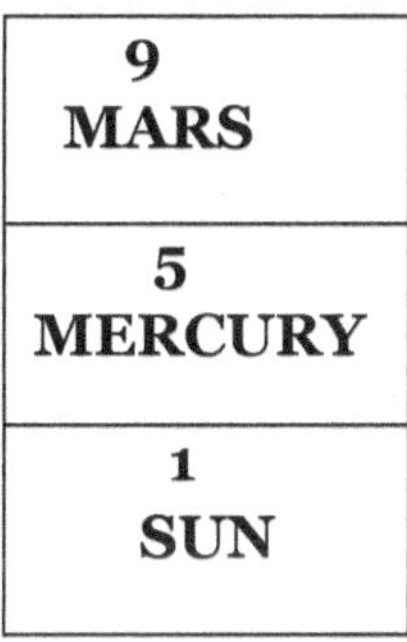

The second vertical line contains 9, 5, and 1 numbers. This plane is called **WILL PLANE.** It indicates that people with a will plane, in their birth chart have very strong willpower. The people are resilient and fighters. In fact, you may say they are real fighters. They are capable of handling the hard situations and bounce back from setbacks. They never bow down to any adverse situations including financial, emotional, or physical situations. They appear very calm from the outside. You can't understand the people by merely seeing their faces.

In this line 5 makes the difference. A line without 5 may not give such balance in life.

| 2
MOON |
| 7
KETU |
| 6
VENUS |

The nest vertical line can have 2,7 and 6. This line is called **ACTION PLANE.** People having this line in their numeroscope are action-takers and industrious. They can achieve their goals by taking timely actions. Once decided they chalk out a plan to execute it. Their lives are full of action, action, and action. For them "impossible is a word that is found in a fool's dictionary."

Now two diagonal lines are left to explain.

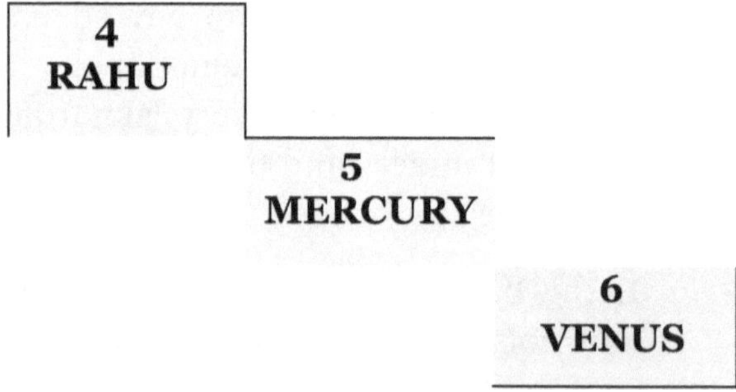

The first diagonal lines are 4,5, and 6, known as the **SUPER SUCCESS LINE.** These number forms a yoga known as **RAJ YOGA** or **GOLDEN YOGA.** In a horoscope, many Yogas are seen. People having this line in their numeroscope are super successful in their lives. They can have names, fame, happiness, and money. No doubt they are action-takers but success touches their feet. They never face major setbacks in their lives. They may or may not born rich but soon rise to name and fame with their luck and endeavors. You may call them lucky champs. They are aggressive, balanced, and rich. Check your birth chart. You may have such a line of supper success.

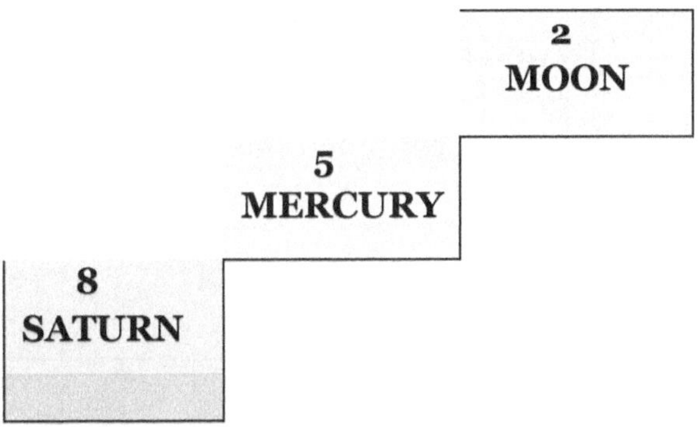

The second diagonal line contains the numbers 2,5 and 8. This line is **CALLED SUCCESS LINE** or **SILVER YOGA.** The people having success line in their numeroscope ought to be successful in their lives. As 2,5 and 8 are earth elements, businesses related to earth like real estate, agriculture, and the stock market can suit them better. They can make a lot of money from such types of business. They can have won a home early. The presence of 8 in this line makes them rich, live in rich and die in rich. They are very patient and wait for the right time to strike. They never lose sight of their goals in any circumstances. You might have such silver yoga, check now.

Now all 8 lines and their importance have been explained. Hope you have understood it better and can able to utilize it for the improvement of your life as well as the lives of others.

SMALL ARROWS

However, everyone is not so lucky to have one or more complete lines. Some people have the following combinations such as 9,7/7,1/3,1/3,9.

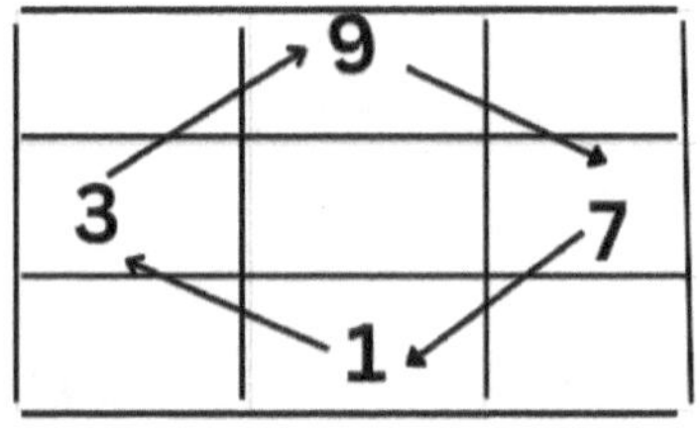

9,7: the presence of 9 & 7 in the birth chart keeps the person balanced in the different situations of life. The person may not lose control over his own sentiments and emotions. He maintains faith in himself and spiritualism.

7,1: The persons with the presence of 7 & 1 in the birth chart are research-oriented people. They go deep into any situation or event to find the truth. They love research.

3,1: It is a combination of the Sun and Jupiter. One is king and another is guru. The people having these numbers in their birth charts are spiritual, knowledgeable, and intelligent. They are good communicators and orators.

3,9: The presence of 3 & 9 in the birth chart makes the person litigant and argumentative. They can't take the thing simply.

What did we understand from the above topic? Each number has energy and vibrates in a frequency. Combinations of two or more numbers create specific energy bonding and vibrate in specific frequencies that influence the life of the people.

Conclusion

The Loshu Grid demonstrates how specific number combinations can influence our lives in profound ways. By analyzing horizontal, vertical, and diagonal lines, we gain insights into our mental capabilities, emotional depth, practical approach, and willpower.

For instance, the Mental Plane reveals brilliance and sharp thinking, while the Emotional Plane highlights compassion and sensitivity. The Practical Plane suggests a logical approach, and the Will Plane shows strong resilience and determination.

Diagonal lines like the Super Success Line and Success Line indicate the potential for great achievements and financial success. Even if your grid isn't perfect, combinations like 9 and 7, or 3 and 1, still offer valuable guidance.

Understanding these number patterns can help you leverage your strengths and address areas for growth, providing a clearer view of your life's potential and direction.

Chapter ten

CONCLUSION

As we conclude this exploration into **"Numerology: A Practical Guide"** it's essential to reflect on the profound insights we've uncovered. Throughout this book, we've cultivated the mystical world of numbers and how they shape various aspects of our lives. From understanding the impact of repetitive numbers to discovering remedies for missing numbers, and from exploring the significance of Yantras to the influence of names and marriage choices, each chapter has offered a unique perspective on harnessing numerological wisdom.

Understanding the impact of repetitive numbers in your numeroscope reveals a lot about your personality and life path. Each number, when repeated, carries its own energy and influence. This can be both a source of strength and a challenge. For instance, a number's frequent appearance can amplify positive traits but might also push certain characteristics to extremes, leading to potential struggles. Recognizing these patterns helps you gain deeper self-awareness, enabling you to overcome life's complexities more effectively. By understanding these influences, you can make more informed decisions that align with your true nature and strive for a more balanced and fulfilling life.

Addressing missing numbers in your numeroscope might initially appear difficult, but understanding the concept of complementary numbers provides balance and reassurance.

Remember every number has a role in shaping your life, and the absence of one number can be counterbalanced by its complementary counterpart. This interconnectedness ensures that even if you're missing certain traits, there are often other numbers that can support your goals. This guide serves as a tool to help you overcome life's challenges and opportunities with greater clarity. Even when certain numbers are missing, there are always ways to enhance and balance your life's energy.

The remedies for missing numbers offer practical solutions to restore harmony in your life. By harnessing the power of elements such as wood, earth, fire, water, and metal, you can fill the gaps left by absent numbers in your numeroscope. Incorporating these elements into your daily routine—whether through wearing specific items or adopting simple practices—aligns you with the natural forces that govern the universe.

These remedies are more than symbolic; they are actionable steps that empower you to overcome obstacles, enhance strengths, and bring a sense of completeness to your life. The journey of personal growth involves taking small, meaningful steps, and embracing these practices can significantly contribute to a balanced and successful life.

Yantras, sacred geometric tools, offer another layer of depth in balancing and uplifting the energies in your numerology chart. Each Yantra, energized with specific mantras and crafted from materials like silver or copper, serves a unique purpose. Whether you seek to enhance core numbers or boost intellectual growth, Yantras connect you with divine energies that can transform your life. By incorporating Yantras and honoring the associated rituals, you align yourself with cosmic forces, taking significant steps toward achieving a balanced and prosperous life.

Numbers are not just digits but fundamental forces that guide our existence. Understanding them involves recognizing both strengths and weaknesses, especially when certain numbers are missing or imbalanced in your chart. Natural remedies offer a practical approach to address these imbalances. Simple actions, grounded in centuries-old wisdom, can bring balance to your life. Whether it's through rituals or daily habits, these remedies nurture your mind, body, and spirit, helping you align with universal energies. This commitment to self-improvement and spiritual growth is a crucial part of your journey toward balance and harmony.

The power of your name extends far beyond mere identification; it plays a vital role in personal and professional success. Aligning your name's spelling with numerological principles can unlock new levels of potential and achievement. While official name changes are not always necessary, updating aspects like visiting cards and social media profiles to match favorable numerological numbers can positively impact your life and career. Embracing the power of your name helps set the stage for a more successful and fulfilling life.

In the context of marriage, whether love or arranged, numerology provides an intriguing lens through which to explore these choices. By analyzing numbers in your birth chart, we can gain insights into the likelihood and stability of different types of marriages. While numerology can offer guidance, the ultimate choice between love and arranged marriage is deeply personal and influenced by various factors, including cultural values and individual preferences. What matters most is the mutual respect, understanding, and commitment you bring to the relationship.

The Loshu Grid, with its specific number combinations, illustrates how different lines can influence our mental capabilities, emotional depth, practical approach, and willpower. Even if your grid isn't perfect, understanding patterns like the Super Success Line or Success Line offers valuable guidance. Recognizing these number patterns helps you leverage your strengths and address areas for growth, providing a clearer view of your life's potential and direction.

As we wrap up this book, remember that numerology is not just about understanding numbers but about using this knowledge to enhance your life. Each concept, from repetitive numbers to remedies and Yantras, offers tools for personal growth and self-improvement. Embrace these insights with an open mind and a willingness to explore how they can positively impact your life. The journey doesn't end here; it continues as you apply these principles and discover new ways to align with the energies that shape your existence.

Thank you for joining me on this journey through the world of numerology. I hope this book has provided you with valuable insights and practical tools to help you overcome life's challenges and opportunities. As you move forward, may you find balance, harmony, and fulfillment in all aspects of your life.

DISCLAIMER

The content of this book **"Numerology: A Practical Guide"** is intended for educational and informational purposes only. While numerology can provide valuable insights and guidance, it should not be used as a substitute for professional advice in areas such as medical, financial, legal, or psychological matters.

The interpretations and recommendations offered in this book are based on traditional numerological practices and are meant to support personal growth and self-awareness. However, individual experiences and results may vary, and the application of numerological principles should be done with care and discernment.

Readers are encouraged to consult with qualified professionals for any specific concerns or decisions that may impact their well-being, health, or financial security. The author and publisher do not assume any liability or responsibility for actions taken based on the information provided in this book.

Numerology is a tool for self-reflection and exploration, and its effectiveness depends on the reader's willingness to engage with the concepts presented. Please use this book as a guide and approach its teachings with an open mind, while making informed decisions that align with your unique circumstances.

Thank you for understanding, and may your journey through numerology be one of discovery, empowerment, and positive transformation.

MAY I ASK YOU FOR A SMALL FAVOR?

At the outset, I want to give a big thanks for taking out time to read this book. You could have chosen any other book, but you chose mine, and I totally appreciate this.

I hope you got at least a few actionable insights that will have a positive impact on your day-to-day life.

Can I ask for 30 seconds more of your time?

I would love it if you could leave a review about the book. Reviews may not matter to big-name authors; but they're a tremendous help for authors like me, who don't have many followers. They help me grow my readership by encouraging folks to take a chance on my books.

To put it straight, reviews are the lifeblood of any author. I feel this book **"UNLOCK YOUR DESTINY WITH NUMEROLOGY"** shall enrich you with some actionable steps.

Please leave your review by visiting the "**Review Section** "of this book's page on this platform.

It will just take less than a minute of your time, but will tremendously help me to reach out to more people, so please leave your review.

Thanks for your support of my work. And I would love to see your review.